MILES TO MISERY

Independently published on AmazonKDP
Text and image copyright © 2024 Jim Rheasons
all rights reserved.

Cover illustration NightCafe

MILES TO MISERY

A true account from a victim of narcissistic abuse.

To Steph and family
and also Peter

And for everyone who has helped and continues to help me along this mind-shredding journey.

Also for other victims of the same.
YOU ARE NOT ALONE.

A SWIFT INTRODUCTION

Just to make things clear, I am writing this purely for others experiencing the damaging effects of having fallen for what is now termed a covert narcissist. When we use the word narcissist, we usually think of someone who is flamboyant in nature, but the covert variety operates under the radar. The longer you are with them, the more chance they have to change your mindset. This does not mean you are weak-minded. They are naturally masters of manipulation and well-versed in tactics to extract what they desire from you. Anything you receive from a covert narcissist will have a purpose that benefits them personally. The chances are, they will almost certainly take it back from you after discarding you from their lives and moving on. I will, of course, be sharing my own experience with such a person. To protect identities in alignment with legalities, I shall be referring to her as Nikki. After this, I will go into an additional part of this book to inform you where I got help when my life was turned upside-down.

I must also stress, I am not a professional writer, and apologise in advance for any typos and grammar mistakes I make along the way.

To my beautiful children, I am absolutely certain that if you ever read this book and figure out my real identity, I wish you to see how long and hard I fought to remain in your lives, despite how chipped my own life became. You are not at fault for any of this, and please do not be cross at your mother either. I love you both; you are my dream come true twofold. You will adapt throughout life and see your own truths. Just know I will be there for you until I pass into the hereafter, like a sanctuary from how things may go between you and Mummy. I hope you profit from this book.
To any film-makers wishing to use my story... I await your request.

Jim Rheasons

So here I am. It is November 27th 2015. I'm tidying the bedroom in a house-share which I rent with two others in Newark. Our combined wages have given us a nice amount to rent a fine house indeed. It has been decorated well and seems very Edwarian. Even the serving bells have been left fixed to a room near the kitchen. But this is 2015, and as I change the substrate in my leopard gecko's vivarium, I ponder at why I haven't met anyone at 39 years of age? Ramona, my lizard, my little companion for 20 years. The song Living A Boys Adventure Tale by A-Ha is playing as I tidy up. I feel certain that I will never find Miss Right, nor become a father. I have had several dates and fleeting romances. Surely someone will have me? I don't drink, smoke, gamble, take chemicals I shouldn't. I know I am not the best looking fellow, but I have a big heart and a loyalty that would probably account for my undoing. I have been on the internet dating site for a while now. Maybe I should just call it a day and embrace a solitary life and freedom from the stresses a relationship could cause?

Especially with my fathers health declining. It is so nice to be able to see him once a week since he moved up here.

"Nobody falls in love faster than a narcissist who needs somewhere to live"
E.S

My Memoirs Begin

N.B. Asterisks will highlight red flags that I missed during the relationship. A section typed in italicised font will explain in further detail. Some of these were even discovered post the discard.

If you'd rather skip ahead to the help section, it is on page 106

Thursday, December 3rd 2015

Another day another dollar. Such a repetitive job cleaning for Royal Mail but I am paid well. The manager can shake her action plans all she likes, I can only do some areas when the postal staff are out. I'm bored right now. Ruth's having her dinner so I don't have anyone to play Left4Dead with just yet. Ill check my phone and see if someone has viewed my dating profile. Nope. Ah well!

The evening rolls on. It's 8PM, I shall give it until 9PM. I turn 40 next year, that'll be the cut off point I reckon.

8:35pm

Zzzzt zzzzt! My phone vibrates. It's a message from the date site. Somebody has responded to my profile.

Well, a lovely conversation with someone called Nikky takes place via the datemail system. Poor thing, she'd in the woman's refuge having fled domestic violence. Has been single for two years. Battling her ex, Paul, for custody of their three kids.* Well, maybe I could be a white knight and invite her out? She's busy tomorrow but can see me on Saturday evening. That ties in nicely as I am going to meet Mark for lunch in the morning. I can devote the evening to her.

I have a date!

We seem to have a lot in common. She is a bookworm – even more impressively, a speed reader. I've always been a gamebook fanatic. She says geocaching sounds like fun as well.

In a world where the mother usually becomes the residential parent, I should have looked further into this. With her being in a refuge her story sounded so authentic.

Saturday, December 5th 2015

Great morning with Mark. We had sticky ribs for lunch and got a few games of chess in. He thrashed me of course, seven games to two. Told him about Nikky and he wished me good luck. She should arrive at 7PM tonight.

7PM
Nobody here yet. 7:15PM – have I been catfished?

7.25PM
I get a text through on my phone. She's out on the street and cannot find the house. I go out to meet her. Nigh time fell hours ago. I'm just wearing jeans and that yellow t-shirt with blue stripes an ex bought for me two years ago when we dated.

There she is! Under the lamppost.
 "Nikki?" I call out.
  "Yes" she responds.

I cross the road and embrace her. She looks

great. Slim, well presented and a tiny bit of make-up on her eyes. She's made an effort and there's me in my casual attire.

We head back inside into the room which doubles as my personal lounge, through the lovely French window. She seems impressed by the chandelier and open fireplace. (Told you it was a nice house.)
She takes a seat next to me on the three-seater sofa and we begin chatting. She tells a pretty convincing story in more detail about her ex being abusive, the one before him a swinger, and the one before him a cheat*

"All I ever wanted was to have children by a good man." She claimed

We must have spoken for ninety minutes and she spins around and straddles my lap as the conversation flags. Over the next part of the visit, intimacy occurs.**

She leaves, promising to come back. She tells me I am a nice person. I leave a positive message on facebook. Something along the lines of 'The world just got that bit nicer.'

*A pattern emerging there?
** On a first date? A narcissist will love bomb you to secure a supply from you. Sometimes it is financial. Other times something else altogether. She told me she knew I was the right person as soon as she met me, regardless of what we had in common. Another thing a narcissist may do is called mirroring, asserting they are into similar pastimes to create a larger but false bond with you.

Monday, December 7ᵗʰ 2015

I hear Nikki's footsteps on the drive as she walks up to the French window and enters the room. I'm so happy to see her. We texted all day yesterday. During a post coital conversation, she tells me that I am a good man and deserve to have children. I must admit, nobody has said they wanted children with me before. She cannot get enough of me. She even speaks of getting married as soon as she can. How we could have our own place. The ceremony could be book themed due to our enjoyment of reading. * This is too good to be true. She has given me some sort of confidence I have never felt before, even though wrestling her ex in family court. She tells me that he was so abusive that she fled with their three children down to this area, but during a failed attempt at reconciliation, he managed to get them back when they moved in with him again. He served court papers so she could not flee with them again. I regale her with how my mother raised me alone after moving me 200 miles away from my father after their divorce. I grew up without him, but 6 years ago, he moved to the area and we formed a good father/son relationship. I told her of how careless mother was with money, and I virtually starved at weekends and was usually dressed in outdated clothes as a child. This got me bullied at school frequently. She listened intently as I spilled my life story.** We share a deep bath together before she goes. I feel incredible.

This is called future faking. Another trust generating tactic which narcissists will exercise. They will promise the Earth and not keep their word. I have always wanted to be wed. She knows it now.

*** Just remember, a sound person will bear things in mind. A narcissist will learn your weaknesses from what you tell them. They will know all the right things to say, and things to do to fill you with trust for them. Beware the word soulmate early on. They will use it to make you think you are utterly important to them as well.*

Friday, January 7th 2016

Nikki seems very keen on the bedroom activities. It seems to be every visit. She says we can get engaged soon, but not married until her divorce comes through. We spend plenty of time together, going to pub lunches, second-hand bookshops, or garden centers. She drives as I am not a driver and I pay for the meals. It's a nice little arrangement. I haven't had this much fun with someone for years. I actually feel like her partner, not a temporary boyfriend. I have met a few of her friends from the refuge at an event too. Ally, Marnie, Alissa. They're such good-looking women. I cannot comprehend men who treat partners so badly. She has another friend who has just moved into the refuge. Her name is Judy but I have not met her yet. There seems to be a good camaraderie among them.

I would later learn Nikki got their approval in her choice of man. This made me feel proud.

Saturday, February 13th 2016

We had our Valentines day early today. Enjoyed a lovely meal together and went geocaching. We took a shortcut through the quarry as Nikki wanted to visit *Go Outdoors* to look at the price of tents. I received my first Valentines card in years. What was written inside blew me away. I don't think I have ever felt this important to anybody I have been with before.

*

> You are my dream,
> my soul-mate,
> my love,
> my Valentine.
> For now and ever more.

Once they have gotten to know you, a narcissist will know all of the things which make you tick and use them to their advantage. They will lay it on thickly too, making your personal barriers come down. You will ultimately become their yes-person, and not see any wrong in what they are doing. Strong barriers are so important no matter how smitten you become with somebody. Before you know it, you begin throwing everything at them to make them happy with reckless abandon.

Friday, February 19th 2016

Nikki sends a photo message. I am thrilled to bits. She has a blue stripe! She is going to make me a Daddy. I still cannot believe how amazing she is. We are now planning to spend the entire weekend together. We haven't gone public with it of course. Too soon.

February – March 2016

I attend as many of Nikki's appointments at the maternity clinic as possible. She is granted a council flat in Hannah Street about half an hour's walk away. It takes a little decorating and I lay carpeting for the first time in my life. Being so tall I get to paint the ceilings as well. Soon we have a little love nest. We are a little concerned with the neighbours. A fishwife downstairs, and the lads next door to her are clearly on pot. The latter do not bother us so much, they keep themselves to themselves. After a couple of scans, we begin telling our closest family and friends the news. We name the embryo 'Peanut' for now.

I feel almost complete. I can't wait for us to get married. We still speak about it regularly. We have even looked at rings. There are some nice ones with runes on them, something we have both been interested in at one point.

Nikki is still fighting against her ex in court. If I can make her just that much happier it will be a good distraction. He sounds like a real piece of work. The husband before him lives about 5 miles away. Tony, a farmer who abandoned Nikki and her first daughter, Colette. I'm told Colette was the result of a one night stand when she Nikki was 15. She had another child by this farmer named Annie, but he never lets Nikki see her. She is almost of age now anyway. It seems that her brother and sister have nothing to do with her. She has had some bad luck with men. I want to be the one to show her we are not all bad.

Tuesday, April 19th 2016

We are absolutely gutted. Crestfallen. We attended the 10th-week scan only to find Nikki had miscarried. I was looking at the ultrasound monitor. There was no flashing heartbeat, no peanut shape, nothing...just darkness. Nikki cried out as the nurse broke the news and I fled to her side. With tears streaming down our faces, we remained in the room to compose ourselves. We needed to walk through an entire waiting room full of expecting couples. They must have known. Nikki called her friend, Robert. Well, her ex-boyfriend from her teen years actually – the one who I had been told cheated on her. He was in a sorry but sober state. Nikki wanted cheering up. He drove us out of town to a Little Chef in Boston where we had a small snack. Our appetites were not up to much. Rob seemed quite nice. Certainly not the type to cheat. I just remember thinking it was nice they had made up. He seemed to approve of me as well.

Tuesday, 26th April 2016

Nikki stayed over last night. As you can imagine, our carnal thirsts had yet to return but at least we had each other in our arms. I was back to work today so got up first to make Nikki breakfast. I heard her yell my name out and went racing upstairs to a fearful sight. Nikki had haemorrhaged from her private quarters. Several palm-sized blood clots lay on the carpet while fresh blood continued seeping over the quilt cover. I suggested an ambulance but she wished to handle this as quietly as possible so as not to attract unwanted attention from the other lodgers. Thankfully the hospital was a short distance away. I stayed with Nikki until the medics were ready to examine her. She promised to message if anything was badly wrong. I confess I got to work late and left early for this reason. Thankfully nobody noticed. I wished to see her during visiting time to make sure she was okay. I bought her a copy of a book I had enjoyed recently – *The Girl With All The Gifts*.

I arrived with 45 minutes of visiting time to spare once I had discovered which room she was convalescing in. The smile on her face when I walked in was pure joy. She was happy to see me and didn't expect that I would visit her. Why wouldn't I? She's my dream come true and been through so much. She has very few friends. It turned out her uterus had become infected after the removal of the miscarriage. She would be fine in a few days and a course of pills.

I wanted to stay but also knew I needed to head home and clean up the mess in the bedroom in case anybody saw it. Thankfully nobody did. I must have spent a good hour just scrubbing the stains that the clots had left on the carpet. The main thing is, she was okay. I was in tears and loaded the bloodied bedding into the washing machine. Somehow we managed to avoid getting caught out in each stage of this crisis. Ruth had met her mother, Susie, after school, and Adrian was still at work. Phew!

Monday, May 2nd 2016

Nikki has at least physically recovered. Such a run of bad luck lately and she informs me that her ex has been bullying her with texts over their court case. She turns the subject to getting engaged. I am overjoyed she has even mentioned it, and we take to the internet looking for a suitable ring. The one she chooses is a mysterious choice. Silver with a Blue John stone inset. Apparently she doesn't like gold and we had both been on school trips in our youth to Treak Cliff Cavern where the stone is mined. It wasn't expensive, so I order it that very day. We both needed something to defy our misfortunes lately, and we had been together just a few days shy of six months now.

Tuesday, May 10th 2016

With the ring arriving, we get engaged. So many people on Facebook congratulate us. My sister, Sue, even sent a bottle of Champagne. She was so happy for us.

Friday, May 27th 2016

It's my 40th birthday. I made it! I found my Miss Right before the big four zero. I am given a surprise party at The Plough in a village called Nettleham. Quite a few family members turn up and meet Nikki for the first time. I am so happy that my Dad can see Nikki has made me happy, especially with his health deteriorating of late. He will be in hospital again soon no doubt, I hope they can do something.

Saturday, May 28th 2016

Nikki drove us out to collect a new pet dog as my birthday present. I cannot keep him at the house share, so he will remain in her flat for when I move in. We call him Nano... a nod to our geocaching antics. A gorgeous black and white Sprocker Spaniel just a few months old. A little disobediant still but he'll come round with training.

Saturday, June 4th 2016

Nikki has arranged to drive up in a van to her ex's in Scotland to pick up her remaining items of furniture. When they arrive back, she stores her heavier furniture at my place as it is too large to get up the flat stairs to the second floor. Nano is apparently staying with Marnie, who has acquired her own place in the area with her son.

Tuesday, June 21st 2016

I leave work and go straight to Nikki's flat, something which has become the norm. She has made a plateful of sandwiches for my return. You could cut the atmosphere with a knife. She tells me she is going back to Scotland to live in a caravan in Paul's yard until she can secure her own place. I am absolutely devastated. When she leaves, she takes Nano with her as well as I am unable to have a dog where I rent. She tells me to give her furniture away.

Saturday, June 25th 2016

My last perception of them is driving away in her silver Audi. I feel as if all of the life has been taken from me. I break into tears at work. Even make plans to follow her up there if just to spend a few hours. She still messages me all of the time. My mood would be low for some weeks.*

A covert narcissist likes to keep their options open. Even when they fall out with you, they may begin texting if things are not working out so they can re-enter your life. This is known as vacuuming.

Sunday, July 17th 2016

Nikki reports that Paul has started being abusive and that the house is a complete mess. She tells me she is returning to the flat before her rent expires. I am ecstatic and say I am ready and waiting to continue where we left off. She returns back on the **28th**, after a 10 hour drive. Nano is not with her. She informs me that she had to re-home him in Fife, as he attacked a neighbours livestock. Whilst this sounds like something Nano may have done, it sounds a little extreme. I am just happy to be a fiancée again.

Sunday, July 31st 2016

Three days later, Nikki drives us out to Snettisham Lavender Fields in Norfolk. With our relationship rekindled, she makes it clear that she wishes me to move in with her as quickly as possibly. Come August the 6th, this would happen. Things appear to be back to normal. My father is back in hospital again. He seems to be passing so much blood along with his urine. We visit him, and even my prodigal sister, Mandy, has shown up on the scene to visit him.

Monday, August 8th 2016

Nikki goes back to Perth to visit her children during their summer holidays.

Saturday, August 20th 2016

I visit my father at the hospital. It is also thundering so I switch my phone off for the two hours I am there. Nikki has gone out with her friend Judy and her two young sons, also from the refuge. When I return, I call out, " I'm back sweetheart." as I enter the flat. I did not expect this reply.

"I don't think you have the right to be calling me that."

What the hell? I walk into the living room and see Nikki seated with a bottle of Chardonnay almost empty.

"Where the hell have you been? Why was your phone switch off. You put the meat in the slow cooker wrong." She yells.

A tirade of verbal abuse continue and she tells me to get out. I call my sister, who picks me up from the flat about an hour later. I haven't even unpacked my possessions since moving in so I shift them all outside the from door ready to load up

Sue's car. She arrives and I have just to fetch my books from the living room where Nikki remains pissed as a fart. Sue follows me in.

"What do you think you are doing?" Challenges Nikki.
"Just getting my books then I am gone like you requested." I reply

She raises to her feet and steps towards me.
"This is my flat, what gives you the right to take things from it."

Sue steps between us and Nikki stifles, "Ya' know what, just go. Get out!"
Probably a wise move. I'm as soft as mud but Sue has been known to knock out men.

I stay at my Dad's place with his partner and waste no time applying for a bedsit. I can't process what and why has happened. I purchase a book, *The House On Cold Hill*, to keep my mind off of things. The following night Nikki gets Marnie to text me an apology. Nikki's excuse is that she has had a breakdown due to how Paul had treated her while she was in Scotland, and that she missed her kids badly. The alcohol brought it all out. *

Two days later, we would meet at a public place for a chat to iron things out. I forgive her. More fool me. Owing to the split, I am now renting a bedsit.

*This was a proper example of being vaccuumed. Once sobered up, she probably realised I was one of few friends she had, and my income was beneficial. Readers beware of this.

Saturday, September 17th 2016

We drive out to Horncastle. A little second-hand bookshop is situated there, where we found some favourites for just a few pennies. After a successful haul of popular titles, we return home. Passion takes over at some point and once again, Nikki takes me to heaven and back.

Tuesday, October 13th 2016

It is confirmed. Nikki is pregnant once again. I am overjoyed, yet a little more cautious this time about passing around the news. Peanut still enters my mind to this day. Nikki purchases herself a kitten. A cute little black and white female which we name Drut after the character on *The Trap Door*. I am an atheist, but even I pray to the universe that this time everything can be ok. Even though I live at the bedsit, I spend most nights at the flat.

Monday, November 7th 2016

Nikki has been told to go back to work while she still can, and gets a position as a call centre assistant for BT. Id meet her at the gates at her home time. We might even nip in McDonalds and I would treat her to a cheeseburger. Meanwhile, I still have my job at Royal Mail. I have held it down for 10 years now.

Wednesday, December 6th 2016

Filled with a nasty cold, I stop at Nikki's flat. I am relaxing in the morning and there is a knock at the door. I scramble to get some clothes on as something is pushed through the letter box. I manage to open the door and meet a man about my age.

"Is Nik in?" He asks
 "No she's at work, can I take a message for you?" I reply.
  "No that's okay." He responds, turning round and trotting down the steps.
   " Who shall I say called?" I call out.
    "Simon!" He shouts back, fast on his feet.

I close the front door and pick the paper up off of the floor thinking it may be a flyer or other advertising. To my surprise, it is a letter from Simon. A very flirty letter saying sorry he had missed her and hopes she will visit again soon. Just....flirtier, with hearts and stuff. This makes me feel uncomfortable. I drop it back beneath the letter flap to see if she would mention it when she returned home. She didn't!

The following Thursday, I notice her texting this Simon out of the corner of my eye. I *would* have left her there and then, but the dynamic was now changed. She was carrying my child. The text she got back said:

Can't wait to see you. Will you be coming in your pyjamas?"

I challenged her about this Simon, who she claimed was just a friend from her school days, and that flirting was just his way. "You can ask Judy if you don't believe me." She barks in reply.

I tell her it was uncomfortable with that kind of communication to which she responds:
"Fine!" and answers Simon saying not to contact her in that manner and why. The evening was rather quiet after this, but I had made my point.

Friday, March 17th 2017

We are laying in bed at the flat. I am reading, while Nikki taps away on her phone. She starts telling me of how she wishes to be back in Scotland near the children again. It pulls on my heartstrings. She breaks it to me she has applied for a flat up in Kintyre. She is carrying my unborn child. I have no choice but to agree to move with her if I am a father. Away from my family, friends and job. My thirty-seven year footprint in Newark coming to a close. It's bloody cheeky, with my father being so ill. At least he is out of hospital now, but will soon be going for treatment for his prostate cancer. I compromise that I can move up with her slightly after she goes up there, I would need to work off my notice. I wish to ensure Dad is OK and hand in notice to my landlord. She agrees to this, begrudgingly.

Drut goes missing. Nikki says she flew out when she answered the door. How did she get past two security doors then?

Wednesday, May 31ˢᵗ 2017

Our first child, Casey, is born in good health. The midwife barely had time to put her scrubs on. She offered Nikki Casey to hold, but she said, "No, give it to Jim." This wasn't quite the reaction I had anticipated but take Casey I did. Nikki would later inform me she said this in case she went into shock whilst holding baby Casey.

I don't know what is is about becoming a father, I just couldn't stop looking at her. My dream had come true. I was a Daddy to a 7.5lb baby girl. Nikki had given me everything I wished for all of my adult life. We would stay at Judy's for the next two weeks having handed the keys back in for Nikki's flat. We introduced her to my sisters and even my mother, who I never did get along with. She was toxic. But this was the moral thing to do. Even though he was ill, my father held Casey, and had photos taken with her. I have never been so proud. At 41 years old, I never thought it would happen.

Sunday, June 11th 2017

My youngest sibling, Sue, and her partner Phil, paid for all of Nikki's belongs and furniture to be taken up to Kintyre. Phil drove the truck they rented packed with the items, and Nikki drove up with me and baby Casey snuggled in the back. She was such a good baby. Not a single cry along the 11 hour journey. We stopped at many a service station to refresh. It was an adventure I shall never forget. I love road trips even if I do not drive.

We reached Campbeltown early the following morning and had a power nap. Thanks to Sue and Phil, we achieved that which would not have been otherwise logistically possible. For the first time, I would be living far away from my family members.*

Narcissists are well known for separating you from family and friends. They can control you when you have nobody but them to rely on. Bear this in mind.

Friday, August 25th 2017

Nikki buys a puppy. A little border collie that we name Magic. She tells me that his mother was found pregnant in the middle of nowhere, tied to a fence.* I love dogs so I am happy about this. She has set the bunk bed up in our three bedroom flat for when her other kids visit. She has made friends with a middle aged couple, Jason and Wendy. Jason is the manager of the local care home. He offers to interview me.

I move in early September. Sue has even bought us new a new tumble dryer. She and Phil have been true heroes.

Bear this in mind for later reference.

Thursday, November 5th 2017

With no other offers in such a small town, I start working at the care home. It is an area I have never wished to work in, but I slowly attune to the new job.

Thursday, 19th November 2017

I receive a phone call from my father's partner. Dad has succumbed to prostate cancer after surgery. A blood clot got into his system and switched out his life during the night before he was going to be discharged. Jason gives me bereavement leave and we house Magic with some neighbours. The three of us go down to Newark for a few days to mourn. Nikki takes Casey back with her two days early. She says she would rather Casey was back home. She continues to message during my stay. She lays it on quite thick that she is struggling to cope and needs me back. She tells me Paul is making her feel anxious and vulnerable. I have no option but to go back early as well. Any good partner/parent would, right?

When I arrive, she seems fine and settled. Just bothered by what she tells me that her ex has been doing.

December 18th-20th 2017

I slip back to Newark alone for Dad's funeral service with Nikki's kind 'permission'. It all goes as well as can be expected. Sunshine in December is rare. Mandy and her fellow turned up. Disappeared straight after without coming to the wake. There are none so queer as folk I suppose. Nikki calls the housing association. She wants out of the flat claiming the neighbours noise is setting her anxiety on edge. Not another move for goodness sake?

Her other three kids are staying over New Year. Lily, Connor, Amber. I've picked up hours at work anyway.

Friday, January 5th 2018

We have procured a 3 bedroom house a couple of streets away. We gradually move in over the month. Jason and Wendy help with the decorating. Love em.

Friday, March 9th 2018

Nikki recently lost the keys to her Audi. For some reason she has it towed away and today procured a little Peugeot 206 so we can still get about. £550. The seller says it may not last too long so get saving for something better.

Wednesday, July 11th 2018

Nikki was not happy. She didn't like that our back garden was a communal route for next door, and that they had been using our drive. Lo and behold, she wished to move again. She would put in for a private flat closer to my job.

During the the other kid's stay, she arranges to go out with them. Before she does, she loses her temper at me, branding me unhelpful and lacking responsibility. I am not entirely sure where this outburst has come from but it left me wondering if I should just leave, not to mention feeling worthless. I took Magic for a very long walk. A message would ping on my phone . A simple sad emoji and more put downs; although less coarse. * I would go back with magic after feeling a little better. The other kids leave at the weekend. Nikki is overly concerned why I do not wish to have my wages paid straight into the shared bank account we opened when I first arrived. I have monthly outgoings, some I have had for years. I am not ready to apply them to an account she has equal power over. I transfer all of my wages but the hundred pounds or so into the joint account. I inform her I have credit cards for when times are bad.

Word Salad is a phrase used to describe a barage of pickled words and phrases that a narcissist will use to disorient you in a conversation.

Friday. July 20th 2018

I return home from night shift to find Nikki in a state. She claims some children had left the shared gate open and Magic had ran off. She managed to catch up with him with Casey. According to her, he had bitten somebody who had threatened to call the police if he was not put down. With Casey now able to furniture-walk, my concern rested with her. If Magic bit her for example, I would never forgive myself. Ultimately, Nikki took us to the vets. In the interests of Casey's welfare, the decision was made to euthanise Magic. A little later, we would acquire two little black kittens. We named them Haggis and Neeps. Casey took to them straight away. Every pet I had ever had was a lifelong commitment. My gecko was about to turn 24 years old. Why is it each pet I have lived with through Nikki has lasted bare months? Jason and Wendy cannot believe we are moving again. I raise concern with Jason at work about it and he guesses she will keep on moving and never be settled.

Friday, July 27th

Nikki falls pregnant with our second child. It's been a bumpy month, but I am absolutely overjoyed once more. Surely I can trust her with anything now? I'd certainly do anything for her now. She has also managed to patch things up with her sister Kate, who live in Cornwall.

Monday, August 13th 2018

We move into the new privately rented flat with the out of the local man-with-a-van. I am off work so assist getting furniture up the spiral staircase. It's a lovely flat. Wooden panelling, open log fire. (Don't worry for Casey, there is a guard.) It is probably this week that I meet Nikki's Community Psychiatric Nurse, Marie. It is rather odd she has one of these for anxiety and depression. Am I not getting the full picture here? Marie is wonderful. Anyone would want her to be their mother if they didn't have one.

December 20th 2018

Apparently the car has been playing up. Nikki is making hints that she wishes to move again. Her reasoning this time is that she wishes to be close to her sister in case anything goes wrong during the pregnancy. She would rather not be airlifted all the way to Glasgow. Surely Wendy and Jason would keep us alright as far as a birthing partner goes? During a meeting, Marie asks why Nikki doesn't have me as her live at home carer. She manages to sell the car.

Sunday, January 20th 2019

Nikki begins telling me that Jason and Wendy have been falling out. He has hit the bottle and smashed up the living room. I knew he liked a tipple but didn't think he had a problem. Someone called Bethany was giving him a hard time due to being fired. Maybe this was the cause? Nikki tells me that at 7 months pregnant and having anxiety, she needs to be away from here.

Wednesday, February 6th 2019

We go to the local Peugeot showroom. They have a second-hand Citroen Picasso for £1500. It looks reliable enough to get us to Cornwall at least. The decision to go has been aided by Marie. All I can hear in my head is 'What if she misses her other kids again?' Anyway, we use my credit card to pay for the car. I am sure she will contribute towards repayments. *

Never do this for anybody. Ever. Her name was not on that card, only mine. Smitten as I was, I would learn a costly lesson here.

Wednesday, February 13th 2019

I have been told to keep this move hush hush, handing in emergency notice to the lady who has taken over from Jason while he is off. We embark on our drive to Cornwall to meet her sister.

Thursday, February 14th 2019

We stayed at a Travelodge in Preston last night to split the Journey, but we make it to Saltash and rendezvous with Kate. They haven't seen each other for years. She has arranged for us to stay at a friend's farm while we apply for emergency accommodation. 625 miles! Even further than the Newark to Campbeltown move. We unload the car and enter the converted barn we would be calling home for the next two months. Nikki receives a text message from Wendy back in Campbeltown. She says it is very negative and I must not speak to Jason if he texts me, he's apparently hit her. My SIM expires soon anyway, so I just purchase a new SIM card and number. Nikki has her iPhone, so operates from two SIMs anyway. *

This is how a covert narcissist can live two lives at once, arranging things without you knowing. Nikki didn't work, she had no reason for two SIM's. I thought nothing of it. I trusted her implicitly by now.

Monday, March 11th 2019

Housing have placed us into emergency accommodation now. A Travelodge in Saltash not far from Nikki's sister. Most or the stuff that we cannot fit in the car has gone into storage. The only way to pay for this is via my credit card. This is about £10 per day, so that plastic is melting.

Monday, March 25th 2019

We are tossed into a holiday park at Trelawne for the next fortnight. Our second child, Tanya, is born healthily six days later. Kate attends to Nikki during the birth at Plymouth hospital while I am back at Trelawne holiday park looking after Casey. I am lucky she is a Daddy's girl. Nikki returns with baby Tanya. I am at the height of my happiness as a multi-child father, something I never thought would happen. There is nothing I would not do for Nikki anymore.

Thursday, April 4th 2019

We are moved into a top floor flat in Liskeard as our list of emergency accommodation expands. We bump into the lady downstairs, Emma, with her two children as we return from the shops. It appears she is in a similar situation, escaping domestic violence. She seems to be an ideal person for Nikki to acquaint with. Over the next 6 weeks we would become good friends. Emma's mother lives on a farm not far away, so she drops us a tray of eggs round once in a while. The flat is nicely modernised with all new mod-cons. Just a noisy area!

Friday, May 17th 2019

We are now moved into a ground floor flat in Truro. I must say, I like it here. There's a park not far away, and Casey if due to start Nursery soon. That is in walking distance as well. The neighbours are a mixed bag but we aren't here to mix anyway.

Friday, May 31ˢᵗ 2019

I cannot believe my little Caseywoo is 2 years old today! Tanya is 2 months old today. We buy cake to celebrate and their Auntie Kate brings Casey a new pet kitty. I not very fond of the whole 'pets as presents' idea, but Casey is very happy. I am not saying we do not like the cat, but it isn't the best time with us being in emergency accommodation. We shall do our best, I am sure. My only gripe is that Kate let her son name the cat. He called her Aura. Nikki is annoyed about this and complains that the cat feels more life it has been dumped on us for Kate's son's sake rather than as a present for Casey.* He seems to be one of those kids that gets their own way. Very spoiled. Sue and Phil would visit for a few days and we would go to St Ives and Looe. Great to see them as ever. Judy and James would also come and visit with their kids. Bless em'.

Maybe this is an early sign that Nikki is'nt as close to her sister as I thought?

Saturday, July 20th 2019

Nikki has been speaking about getting a dog for some time. We purchase Libra, a beautiful English Pointed from a local specialist breeder, Steph, for £900. I pay, Nikki signs the contract as Libra is a KC registered pup. We get her microchipped and she is a wonderful addition to the family. She also gets along with Aura. She is such a good puppy and makes only two floor mistakes. Pointers are my favourite breed, I bond with Libra immediately.

August 2019

Casey begins nursery school. Nikki pokes fun that I am shedding a few tears. This is the first time I have known her to be away from both of us.
It is one night after this, I am awaken by Nikki speaking to her sister on the phone. Being night time, I can hear every word her sister is saying as well as they exchange conversation. Apparently, Nikki's other

nephew has had car troubles and he needs some money fast.

"How much, I can transfer some." Asks Nikki, blissfully unaware I have been awoken,

"Four hundred. He says he can pay it back with his wages next month." Kate replies.

"I'll send it over now..."

" Shouldn't you clear it with Jim first?"

"No, it doesn't matter. This is my disability money...."*

I played dead, wondering why all of a sudden her "disability money" wasn't "family money" anymore.

*This was another huge red flag, deliberately ignore solely because I trusted her so implicitly now. One thing is for certain, my boundaries has been destroyed.

Monday, September 2nd 2019

The local housing association had finally found us a place which they deemed 'suitable'. We would be moving back to Liskeard to a street called Bodgara Way. While the house was ok-ish, we had arrived at Chav Central. Thankfully we were dwelling at the far end of the street which backed onto a woods and farmland. Ideal for walking Libra. I do confess, Nikki had to do this move with 2 removal men as I had gone to a convention in London for four days. She didn't seem to mind although it would come back as petty swipes if she tried to argue against me. She seems to be forgetting exactly what my family and I had done for her over the past three years.

Saturday, October 5th 2019

Nikki's friend Marnie and her son come to stay with us, clearing it with me first. She was facing a rough neighbourhood back up in Newark. Jealous wives etc not liking her speaking to their husbands. Marnie had done so much for Nikki in that refuge, and when she had the flat after leaving it. What we didn't count on is Marnie also brought her Staffy with her. We needed to keep her away from Libra, and suddenly found ourselves unable to have our dinners at routine times due to Marnie inhabiting the kitchen at the same hour. After four weeks, Nikki informed me that Marnie was rejecting places being offered to her as a home. She also accused Marnie of trying to groom me, based on her buying me a chocolate bar, and a flatcap which matched one she bought for her son. Ultimately Nikki put of quite a display, and if having a nervous breakdown. I had never actually 'seen' her act like this before. Tears, screams, avoidance. Marnie must have felt awful. She would leave in November after five weeks with us. As much as I tried to keep peace, she never spoke to her again. I was also told to block contact.

It was around this time Nikki received a

benefit backdate of £2500. She had the opportunity to pay back about two thirds of the credit card money which had covered our way here. She used the entire lot to buy stair carpeting. I must admit, this observation pissed me off somewhat. But she said it was "to make our forever home look nice."

Thursday, January 16th 2020

With the stairs carpeted and hallway painted, the place was feeling very homely. I would walk Libra daily in the woods and through the farmland. I indulged in a little seed-ball bombing along the way. Casey had settled into Rising Stars nursery, but Tanya had picked up a bug recently which lasted for ages. Weeks in fact. As she slowly recovered over the month, the TV news was beginning to fill with reports of a super virus. I hope Tanya hadn't contracted this... if she had, we were lucky to still have her.

Monday, February 10ᵗʰ 2020

Nikki expresses a desire to move – yet again – back to Kintyre on the grounds that her sister had become overbearing and verbally degrading. If we had to move back, it would certainly be the last thing we could do. Everything would need to be paid for on credit and mail order. Since I was the only one who had this kind of credit behind me, it would all be on my accounts. She said that once settled, we could consolidate everything and pay it back that way. We were a family after all. I was sceptical, but this woman had given me two daughters, Any amount of bed exercise, and been with me longer than anybody else by this point. She regularly said, "Now do you believe I am here forever, darling man?"

Even though I wanted to stay, the house did have its downside. Black mould grew into the kitchen wall, and after heavy rain, water would seep into the lounge via the skirting board. I couldn't really say no. We stayed in touch with Emma all this time and said our goodbyes. We would keep in contact thanks to social media. Nikki apparently rehomed Aura at a home in St Cleer, but we took Libra with us. Nikki had managed to find us a place in the village of Tayinloan, just twenty miles away from Campbeltown. I was worried how our return would go down if we encountered Jason and Wendy. I was Nikki's carer now so did not really need to work. It was nice to feel wanted and valued. Little did I know it was a sham.

Saturday, February 29th 2020

We made it to Tayinloan... just! The Citroen has broken down near the Scottish border and we were towed the rest of the way over many more hours than we'd intended to take. At least we arrived safely. The girls had been little angels, largely sleeping most of the way. We needed to stay at Big Jessie's Tearoom for two nights as we didn't get the keys to the house until late and the journey had worn us out. I would purchase all white furniture with my Littlewoods account and as for my credit cards... they were all but nuked. We would have a bare minimum of stuff. Still, it is a nice village, set back from the main road. A nice bit of beach, but we were all now reliant on Nikki. She was the driver.* Thankfully the car got one last repair.

Isolating us again. Do you see the pattern emerging?

Saturday, March 14th 2020

The dreaded super virus had spread far and wide. The government declared Britain to go into Lockdown. Coronavirus aka Covid19, had spread throughout the world killing many with underlying health issues. You could only go out if necessary; and even then not without a face mask. A six foot personal space distance needed to be maintained.

Monday, April 6th 2020

The car is still having troubles and after an M.O.T. Nikki is told it needs two new tyres. Well I have no money left apart from the meagre carers allowance which is going on paying back the creditors. She tells her old teacher, Mick, who has remained her good friend and supporter for many years. He takes pity and sends Nikki £400. It is around this time her other kids are coming to stay. She uses the money Mick has gifted her to buy an Xbox for her son. How can this be right? That money was sent for a specific reason. * My card for the joint account expires in a year. Nikki is in full control of all income but my carers allowance. I trust her. More fool me.

Little signs begin to swell in your gut instinct. Even though she eventually bought the tyres with her next benefit, the action seems immoral. Although this wasn't a sign of what would become of me, it was certainly another signal she wasn't as faultless as I believed her to be.

Monday, April 13th 2020

More drama. Nikki went to pick the other kids up and Paul was running late. By the time he had got there and dropped them off, Nikki had a flat tyre. Looks like the poor car is on it's way out. Thankfully they got back after some help from the AA. We ended up replacing it later in the year with a Vauxhall Zephyr which was equally as unreliable. It is all that we could afford on the meagre savings we had scraped by selling whatever clutter we could put on eBay. She has become very pally with Leigh and Pat. They seem nice enough but very good at telling us who we should not mix with in the village. Can't we find this out for ourselves like everyone else?

Sunday, April 25th 2021

The past year seems to have gone okay, and covidiosy has fallen in the wayside with the inoculations to combat it. Nikki has noticed a few neighbours who we initially bonded with have removed us from their Facebook friends list. She discusses this with Leigh over a cup of tea and Leigh says they are always doing that to her and then re-adding her. She says they are not worth bothering about, and the man and son has verbally intimidated her at her doorstep. All I wanted was a quiet life. I have never been interested in street politics that I am not involved with.

Saturday, August 21st 2021

Lily, Connor and Amber are back with us for a stay. It is during this time that Lily tells her mother that she wishes to come and live with us. She is 16 now so certainly allowed to and welcome in my eyes. I have noticed Nikki has started chatting a lot to John, the old man around the corner. Apparently his Auntie May is on a rapid decline in health. He's over 65 so she must be well old. Is that empathic concern Nikki is displaying? I like to think so. He looks identical to my late father in every way.

Friday, September 10th 2021

Everything has been arranged by Nikki to drive out the Perthshire and pick up Lily. They will meet up during her school lunch hour. I have been left with Tanya and a neighbour shall be dropping Casey back after school.

It seems to go smoothly and they arrive back around 6pm. It is shortly after I am realise they have not told anything about this to the school or Paul. For their own sake, I insist Lily informs the police what she has done, for if I was in Paul's boots I would be incredibly concerned. Lily is of age however, and here of her own will. I do not get to challenge that. At least they listen to my advice. I do not like this though. It was done covertly and immorally in my opinion. All of our existing debts have been consolidated. Instead of paying out £200+ we are only paying out £80. I give Nikki half of my carers allowance now. The rest goes on outgoings I had before we even met. Insurances, pensions, etc.

Wednesday, October 20th 2021

Our relationship seems to be polarising to what it was initially. Sex has not been such a part of our routine this past year. Today would be the last time Nikki and I were intimate.* She is spending a lot of her time around at the old man's place while I am left at home with the girls. Lily only seems to leave her room when it is beneficial... meal times for example. While I do not mind, I have noticed that she leaves a lot of her dinner and then raids the cupboards.

**I dismiss my suspicions. Surely the woman that has been with me for so long, had my children, and been aided by half of my family would not do that? Surely?*

Wednesday, November 10th 2021

We take Casey and Tanya to the play park which is in a field next to John's home. I am with Casey at the slide, and Tanya is with Nikki. I see John walking over and say hello to him as he walks by, hoping to strike a conversation. He reciprocates the greeting but continues walking over to Nikki. They are only seven yards away but he stops and engages in conversation with her for around two minutes. They are standing very close, yet I cannot hear what they are saying. He is also shadowing her every step. I take a discreet photo with my phone camera. Am I letting my pessimism get the better of me?* After about two minutes he walks away and passes me again saying something about the weather before going back inside his house.

My common sense had clearly been restrained by all of the loveliness Nikki had shown me before. This was the beginning of the end for me.

Thursday, December 23rd 2021

Nikki has been on her phone an awful lot. Who is she texting? Not who I might think!

Sunday, December 26ᵗʰ 2021

Nikki tells me that she is concerned with Amber. Nikki has been told by her that her father was being abusive, and that he has grabbed hold of her. Nikki has told me Amber called the emergency services. I cannot believe what I am hearing. Amber took to me more than the other two it must be said, so I would welcome her to a safe home. Amber was dropped off up near Inverary where Nikki went to collect her. Paul gets taken in by the police but there is absolutely no evidence supporting the claim. Something didn't ring true for me. Why wasn't Connor taken from Paul as well? Amber wouldn't say boo to a goose. Reporting her Daddy like that seemed quite sophisticated for a 13 year old with behavioural issues. Truly, she breaks down at the slightest things. I visit a couple of friends we have made over the last year with Nikki for the final time. Janey and Joe. Seem like salt of the Earth people even though I've only visited four short times. I would be wrong.

Wednesday, February 16th 2022

Amber was officially living with us now. Connor still visits during this time when his school holidays tally. Nikki's attitude towards me has changed so much. In the morning after dropping Casey off at nursery, she goes straight around John's until lunchtime. I am left to care for Tanya and Amber who is yet to attend any school. I make their breakfasts, snack and lunches. After the girls go to bed she will go to John's as well. She has even started taking Libra for evening walks claiming she wishes to lose weight. Whenever she is at home I am now usually devalued for something. She doesn't even hold my hand in bed anymore. It was one of our 'personal trademarks'.

Monday, March 14th 2022

Nikki has started playing some really dreary songs on loop while we all have breakfast. I Wish I Never Met You by Dido, and some maudlin country-style song about a guy wishing his cheating ex would return so he could see her while he dumped her all over again? What kind of way is this to start the day, not least in front of children? She has taken over many of the chores I do now, even taking the wheelie bins out. I am still doing the washing up though, and of course looking after the girls when she's around at the pensioners house. Neighbours have come up and warned me he isn't trustworthy. Nikki informs me he had an industrial accident in which he received lots of compensation. Bit personal for just friends isn't it. My mind is so cloudy right now. The person that couldn't praise me enough to people had become distant and even began to beat me down emotionally. I needed to speak to someone... but who? I was reliant on Nikki at this remote and isolated address. The car has also broken down. Joe, Leigh have started taking the girls to school for us. How do we get our shopping? You guessed it...John drives Nikki back and fourth. As for me, she won't even let me do the gardening anymore.

Friday, April 8th 2022

Sue and Phil come to visit, staying for a couple of nights at the tearooms. They have brought us probably £200 worth of shopping in the car. There is so much. Our food cupboards are more than filled. Among the food is two bottles of wine and a box of chocolates.

"These are for you and Jim to have a romantic evening together." Sue says as she holds them up for Nikki to see.

"They're Jim's!" Comes her blunt reply. Somehow her eyes look different. Piercing but hollow, and her smile seems painted on to a face which does not match it.

Sunday, April 10th 2022

It has been great having Sue and Phil stay, and the girls have enjoyed time with their Auntie and Uncle. To her credit, Nikki cooks them a meal this evening which is their dinner before heading home tomorrow. Afterwards, Lily and Amber go up to their room and Nikki puts the girls to bed at the normal time of 7pm. She then asks Sue and Phil to excuse her as she is going for a walk over on the beach, such is her new regime to lose weight. We chat as normal but I am dying to speak out. Do I have that inside me? Sue is my sister, and always been my closest relation. I shall!

"Have yo noticed anything different about Nikki. Her manner towards me for example?" I enquire.

Both of them give a resounding yes, and Phil responds in full.
"When Lily called for help in the kitchen and you brought two plates through. Nikki asked where you got them and you

answered from the kitchen. Her face looked like thunder. Then she dressed you down saying you didn't know who's plate was who's."

"She also gave a sharp look at Phil earlier on."Added Sue.

"I tried to speak to her in the back garden at she was showing me where she had cut the lawn back. Then when you offered to weatherproof the garden take and snapped 'Do you want to do it or do you want it done properly!' Was almost like a temper " Phil recalled.

I had my witnesses. One of the things Nikki hated was that Phil knew her ex husband Tony the farmer from a work job years ago. They'd had a daughter together named Annie, but he had kept her when Nikki and he split up. I do recall Annie getting in touch with Nikki once. Something about buying her a handbag if I recall. I had never spoken to her though, unlike Collette who I did say hello to while her mother webcammed with her during the lock down. She was grown up and working in London though. Made something of herself most admirably. I hope Annie had too.

Anyway, we make a contingency that if the worst did happen, Sue and Phil would come and collect me. At least I would have a roof over my head.

A few days later, Casey would be ferried to nursery in Joe's car, but he had something important that day so Nikki told me Casey would be brought back by him at lunch time. Why she couldn't be in for her children for once is a mystery I may never know the answer to, but this even would be nearly as valuable to be as the aforementioned contingency plan.

Saturday, April 16th 2022

I tell Nikki I have purchased the girls some Easter Eggs for next weekend. She goes living and calls me a waste of money because she has purchased them to. More devaluing and degradation. I constantly feel like I am walking on eggs shells. I don't even know what I am allowed to do or not in my own home or for my own children anymore. It was Tanya's third birthday recently. I bought her a play tent but hid it until after for fear of being called bad. Even Janie and Joe are avoiding me on social media. *

This would later tell me Nikki had started a hate campaign. The infamous Discard Phase was certainly in place.

Tuesday, April 19th 2022

Nikki and I were chatting about how we couldn't afford a car. She was bigging John up about how nice he was chauffeuring her to the shops and other places to get gravel for the patio. I mentioned Joe had been a star as well, when he drove Casey back. She informed me he would be again to which I asked, perhaps jokingly, if it would be another half day. Her face was stern.

"Of course it won't be a half day. Why would it be a half day, Casey has never had a half day." She blurted.*

I froze at the thought of another verbal onslaught headed in my direction. Then something amazing happened which bailed me out. Amber had overheard her mother from the hall and raced into the lounge with us calling, "Yes she did mum, Joseph brought her back at lunchtime last week!"

There was no answer from Nikki who quickly left the room.

I now know I was being lied to. How many more had she told? This type of lie is a perfect example of Gaslighting. I had lived that reality and she had tried make me think it had never happened.

Wednesday, April 27th 2022

Another evening without Nikki. She comes back from John's claiming that she has had a heavy period and just wishes to have a bath and go to bed. I don't object. What I do remember though is that when I do the laundry the following morning her black leggings and underwear are indeed stained, but with the entirely wrong colour for a period. More a sort of 'male grey' stain against her black clothes. I know what is going on but not only am I in denial, the only thing I can do is continue and hope I am not right as I do not have anyone to confide in who may help. If I kicked her out, I would look like the abuser. Lily and Amber would also need to go as I am no relation. Also, how would I support my children? I do not drive. I have been taken advantage off and played in a big way to the point I cannot help myself.

Friday, May 6th 2022

After the usual school run with Casey, Nikki and Lily – who is off for some reason – return Home. I had just vacuumed and mopped through the house. As they enter the door I here Nikki mutter to Lily to have a bath while she sorts things out. I sit with Tanya, I know what it coming next. Those telltale words "We need to talk." were heading my way. The person that had promised me a happy ever after, bore my children, and had until only recently claimed to have loved me unconditionally was about to ditch me.

She asked me to sit at the table with her, and bold as brass said she wanted me to leave the house. She told me I was no good, she needed a man who could take charge. Ummm... did she forget everything me and my family had done for her. She also told me not to speak to Amber about it. I told her to wait while I phoned Sue, saying plans had been made because we had notice her growing increasingly volatile towards me. That once very adoring face turned devilish now, and her voice became more of a frustrated yell. I told Sue that we were right, and the break had happened. She arranged to come and pick me and whatever possessions I could fit into the car up in three days time. I wish I could have taken the girls. I did not have the means and Sue did not have the space in her home to cater for that. Casey was also in school. I did not wish to subject them to yet another move. My credit cards had been drained. I had nothing but what I could carry, and not even carers allowance from today.* My lived had been smashed. I could only eat one meal that entire weekend, as for sleep, no chance. I wanted to stall leaving my children without sleep, even if they wasn't awake. Precisely six and a half years after we first met, it was over and Nikki was unmasked. I would play dumb as to what I knew she was up to with geriatric John. He was the next victim now.

She had lined John up as a new supply, having learned of his compensation.

Saturday, May 7th 2022

I stand in the front garden watching Nikki drive off with John for shopping. If they knew I knew, I would probably tear him a new arsehole. Stay calm Jim...he doesn't know what she will do to him. That shall be his karma.

Tears streamed down my face as Pat walked by. She bid me good morning but stopped as she noticed me crying. She asked what was wrong and I explained how Nikki had dumped me and I was leaving the village as I had nowhere else to go. She seemed to take pity on me, and invited me around later that day for a cup of tea and to chat. She assured me that she was completely unbiased and anything I said would be confidential. During the chat, I told her about the neighbours coming up to me and saying John was cuckolding Nikki. I didn't tell her what I had found in the laundry, but she said as nice as John was, she didn't trust him as far as she could throw him. To try and cheer me up, she invited me and Casey to the park with her granddaughter Ariel. We could chat longer while they played together. So this happened. Pat took a lovely photo of me and Casey. Of course, Nikki absolutely tore into me for not taking Tanya as well when I returned. Given she was spending most the time with John rather than me or her own children I did have to bite my tongue. Even now she was verbally smashing my self-esteem. I notice Joe had blocked me on Facebook. Odd? Janie was still following but not responding to my reply on her wall from last night. In fact, she had deleted the thread today. I got a very strange feeling about them. I hear John's Auntie May had died.

Sunday, May 8th 2022

Horror of horrors, I seem to have misplaced my wallet. I take Libra out across the grazing fields to look. No luck. On the way back I bump into one of the neighbours who had alerted me about John. I explained to them what had happened and they told me to fight back and stand my ground. I filled them in on what had been arranged and why I could not fight back. I would not be able to take the girls to school, there were no jobs in the area, and that Nikki had mental health problems. Of course, she was hiding what they actually were. Now I didn't even have my I.D. thanks to losing my wallet.

I had spent a lot of yesterday packing my stuff. There is no way I could take all of it. Nikki said she could keep the rest for me in the storage space. Finally, a bit of heart? The plan was I would apply for a place back here somewhere and I could see the girls weekends and half of the school holidays. I am a martyr for keeping texts, instant messages, emails etc. I still have this agreement from her to this day. Post split, I recorded every single phone call as well. She would only let me call the girls on a Saturday at 6pm. She claims it was to help them adjust to me not being around.* Hold on a moment, was I not supposed to be coming back? I later saw Nikki out the front sitting inside John's car. I went out there. You should have seen the look on her face when she saw me coming. Her eyes bulged with guilt and she flew out of the car door. I didn't care. I simply went to John's side and told him I was sorry to hear about his Auntie May. He simply replied, "Thank you. Right, I'm going." and drove away. Nikki just stood there as I walked past and returned inside. She asked Amber to share her bed that last night. I had one final night on the settee. No sleep of course, just a final cuddle with Libra.

Monday, May 9th 2022

The day has come. I am an absolute wreck. Nikki takes Casey to school in John's car and then spends half the morning with John while I share the last few hours with Tanya at home. Surely they know I know by now. Amber and Lily are at their school in Tarbert. Nikki arrives home and tells me she is going to Joe and Janie's. Some coincidence that is eh? Just her way of avoiding confrontation when Sue and Phil arrive. My last moment with Tanya is her being plucked up by her mother telling me that I am a complete waste of money. WHOA! Who the Hell's money has she burnt out? Not just mine, but my family's as well. If we were so low on cash, why did she integrate two teenagers into the house and make arrangements to have a log burner installed? How did she pay for the five shelf freezer Janie had sold her a few months earlier?

Sue and Phil arrived and we loaded up the car. All I could think of was my daughters along with a thousand other ruminations at once trying to comprehend what on Earth had happened. Was I really a bad person? How could somebody who up until eight months ago could not praise me enough to people. I don't like profanity, but this was the ultimate headf*ck. The rain would pour down virtually all of the drive home. My senses were shot to pieces.

Tuesday, May 10ᵗʰ 2022

I waste no time in applying for a new accommodation back up in Kintyre. Have not slept a wink, my mind is alive with rumination, like a swarm of bees buzzing inside my head looking for a way out. I stay mostly in my room and I discover I have developed a fear of distance. If I just stay in my room, it doesn't acknowledge my little girls are hundreds of miles away beyond the distant horizon. I emerge from my room for lunch and dinner which Phil makes for me. At least that's two meals. I've also developed a habit of raking my fingernails across the skin on my thumb. The skin dries and peels. I cannot write with a pen as my fine-motor skills have become twitchy. I am not in a healthy way. Is this all a nightmare? Will I wake?

I also get straight on to the government site to organise benefits until I can find an income. I have been commissioned to write a book for a four figure amount. That's something in the bank at least. I also arrange child maintenance immediately.

Wednesday, May 11th 2022

Oh my life! I receive a call from Casey's headteacher saying Nikki had tried to switch Casey's surname to her own maiden name. Now I knew this was a personal attack, as she had tried to convince Lily to do the same when she moved in. It seems since she got her and Amber back from Paul she no longer had any interest in him. I was her new target of hate. I took the liberty of mentioning this on Facebook. It surprised many people as until this point I had said the split was amicable. Almost predictably, I found Janie had now blocked me. No matter how involved they were in this, they were definitely in on it. Knowing of Nikki's past antics with Paul, the truth was spelled out before me. She had fled with Paul's children before he managed to get them back. I was damned if I would let her do this to mine. I sought mediation, which Nikki refused later. They said they couldn't do anything without her cooperation so could draft a paper supporting me to take legal action in

Family Court. My lawyer friend in London told me, "You had better do it sooner rather than later. The longer you leave it, the less likely your chances." It was sound advice. I had led a blameless lawful existence, I didn't know what to do other than email out to as many solicitors in Scotland as I possibly could. I have informed Nikki's CPN that we are no longer an item.

Friday, May 13th 2022

Pat has returned my wallet. Apparently a local found it in the park so I must have dropped it when we went there. She has been a good listener.

Saturday, May 14th 2022

I get to speak to Casey. It seems to last all of a few minutes. How does one keep a 5 year old speaking on a phone for any great time? Over the course of the next week Pat seems to respond less and less.

Thursday, May 19th 2022

I send a message out to Pat. It isn't answered until late, claiming she had been to the cinema to see a film. I reply "Nice, was it anything good?" ...then came nothing. I would be contacted by another neighbour saying that Pat had been seen going into Nikki's. We deduced she wasn't as unbiased and confidential as she claimed. In speaking with many other neighbours, I discover she was the last person I could have trusted. Damn her!

Friday, June 10th 2022

I call Nikki. I record the call for my own sake. She tears into me for trying to get mediation involved and rants about trying to change the girls surnames was a perfectly fine thing to do. I say about my concerns moving up, during which she threatens there is nothing to stop her moving away if I did. A direct threat to my daughters relationship to me.

Thursday, June 23rd 2022

I receive an unexpected Facebook message from somebody who was totally unexpected. Annie, Nikki's daughter from her first husband. She had noticed my blog by chance, and had been following some of my time with Nikki. She used the blog to keep up with pictures of Casey and Tanya. She tells me her mother has virtually abandoned her to move to Scotland. I pointed out about Nikki and the time Annie had asked her to buy a bag. It turns out Annie had been driven from her home and needed money for food . A lot came out in this conversation. The word narcissist was mentioned and I began to look up clips. Through Annie, I was also prompted to contact Collette and Paul, which I did in due course. Oh, did I learn an awful lot. Annie, if you know you know.... your message was so important and prompted me to take legal action as soon as I could. Also, you unblinkered my eyes. I started going outside again. Just that chat with you cured an awful lot. Forever thanks X

Friday, June 24th 2022

Another promising day. Legal action has been secured as I qualify for Legal Aid.* Sadly nothing can go ahead until I am back up in Scotland. Come on Housing do me proud for those daughters. I recently sent some clothes for the girls. I received a very terse message from Nikki saying I was wasting money again. She is still trying to program a false picture of myself within my head, but I have recently found a channel on YouTube about covert narcissism. Each video I watch demonstrates something that Nikki has done to me. NPD – narcissistic personality disorder. This is a thing! I have been duped by a veritable nut case, and from what I would learn, since day one.

Several neighbours have got back to me confirming John has told them he and Nikki are an item. The also share screenshots of Janie and Pat slamming me on social media with Nikki's false allegations. Nikki had conned me for sure, but now had Pat, Leigh, Janie and Joseph acting as her hate spreaders.** Pat's betrayal hit hard, but the rumours what they were putting out about me needed chasing up. Eventually I would get every proof to show these rumours were all lies. Good job too.

**I got lucky. Had I have been working I would not have been able to get Legal Aid. One of those cruel loopholes in the law which leave many alienated parents powerless.*

*** A covert narcissist gives such a sob story that people fall for their crap. We can see in Janie's statement that Nikki had said much to damn my character, and long before I left. Notice her please of ignorance to disassociate her involvement in this screenshot. I am a tall man. I wouldn't eat potato-peel soup for anybody. And what did Janie think we stored in the freezer Nikki bought from her? A ton of King Edwards?*

> His sense of entitlement is amazing. When I found out (on top of everything else) he'd been withholding all his money and using it to buy things for himself while she made potato peeling soup for the family out of desperation, my jaw just hit the floor. Absolutely stunned is an understatement. I cannot understand how someone could do that. All respect for the fella totally gone. I get angry just thinking about it. Xx
>
> 5 w   Like   Reply   2

(?) August 2022

It appears Nikki had lied so much about Paul. All he ever did was take a pay cut to study for a doctorate. He had asked Nikki to get a small job to make up the hours. Two days later, he came back from the shops and Nikki had fled with his kids down to England. I was damned if I would let her do this to my girls and me. He also informed me that she had taken his dog

Hera out one night and failed to return with her. Nikki claimed that Hera had fled. Within the hour he saw Hera's picture on a lost and found post. She had been discovered 20 miles away tied to a fence. De ja vue anyone? I remind you of when she got our previous dog, Magic. She has closed down the joint account now and claimed the consolidators have split the bill.

An apartment had been found for me down in Campbeltown. This was ideal in the fact it had a bus service. By now, Jason and Wendy had been in touch after hearing on the grapevine what had happened. They were incredibly forgiving. I hope I can be if Janie and Joe ever suss it out. Absolutely not for Pat though. She had done a lot of damage and willingly so, even throwing in her own fictional pieces for good measure.

> Stage and screen certainly missed out on this one! An Oscar winning victim performance hooked me line and sinker and has left me feeling manipulated and emotionally abused. I don't say that lightly as I am, in general, a pretty tough

Friday, August 12th 2022

Sue and Phil had been the true heroes. They got me back up to Kintyre and even purchased all of the basic needed furnishings. A social grant paid for carpeting, and the rest of what I had would help make a room for my daughters to stay in. Jason and Wendy came to see me. I didn't deserve their forgiveness, but may I learn from it.

Here I am again. 450 miles from friends and family in Newark. Stuck in a town which just reminds me of when I was happy, like a tormenting thorn in my side. I go out very little because of this. Jason tells me to apply for my old job again. My head is a mess. My mood frequently plummets leaving me in a pool of tears. I am calling helplines frequently. Maybe the job will help keep my mind off of things even if it is part time.

I inform Nikki and finally tell her I know

about her and John. She tells me never to contact her again except through legal field. Bit of an over-reaction for the result of her own actions*

**A narcissist cannot take accountability for their actions. They consider themselves far too perfect and never wrong. It is like holding a crucifix to a vampire.*

Monday, September 5th 2022

Tonight I return to my old job. It is good to see some familiar faces but once again, this is a nod to happier times. I am certainly not as confident or comfortable as I was. Should I have gone back to work so soon? There is still the court to get through, and now Nikki will not let me see my children. The next few months would be the biggest emotional torture I have ever been through. She is doing this out of pure hate. Neighbours tell me they have seen her throwing out my possessions. The bank re-opens our joint account to print off statements, they prove I did not touch a penny of the money other than my personal outgoings. In fact they prove she had a large chunk of my carers allowance per month. Clearly she wanted everything, and with her having an affair in place, would have discarded me anyway.

I begin to see my old neighbours. All but four have either remained neutral or been so helpful. Brionny has become my strongest support, keeping in touch daily. Although we only saw each other a couple of times as she and her husband Dennis walked the dog, she had believed my story due to the huge amount of proof I had shared to back up my claims. Other people including staff members of the girls school had been supportive, one even confirming John as a womaniser. He used to stalk her mother apparently. Looks like they will be each other's karma. Maggie and many more showed concern and support at least for the girls. I shall be forever grateful. They'd seen me out with the dog and girls far more than Nikki after all.

Wednesday, September 7th 2022

My Initial Writ is handed in to court by my lawyer. I pursue that an interdict is placed on Nikki after her telephone threat to relocate, and state that the children are better of living with me than her given Nikki's transient lifestyle. I have been keeping in touch with Emma. She has come forward with screenshots of Nikki giving her a different reason for our break up that what she has told Janie. Caught in another lie, I had everything I needed to prove her manipulation now too. Not a hint about potato-peel soup of spending all the cash.

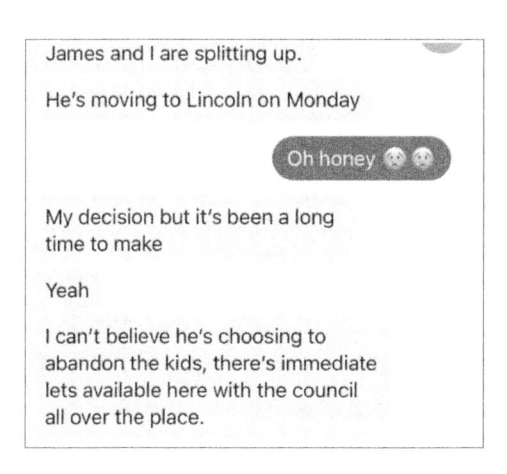

> James and I are splitting up.
>
> He's moving to Lincoln on Monday
>
> Oh honey 😢😢
>
> My decision but it's been a long time to make
>
> Yeah
>
> I can't believe he's choosing to abandon the kids, there's immediate lets available here with the council all over the place.

Emma shares that Nikki blocked her before she got to chat about it properly. She knew that I would never ever willingly leave my children. The fact I hadn't seen them for so long was effecting my mental health. This psychological abuse wouldn't stop any time soon either. I missed Casey's first day at school. A neighbour told me to go out and get a local paper as Casey had had her photo put in it. God bless whoever did this. Would I ever see them again?

Tuesday, October 4th 2022

Letters from debt recovery agencies like Moorcroft were starting to come through the door. The consolidators had not "split the bill" like Nikki had previously said. They were all after me. This added to the turmoil. My life turned from a nightmare to a holiday in hell. Sleep was still just a few hours, I was still on two meals a day, certainly only went out for work and shopping purposes so my physical health was also diminished.

Monday. November 14ᵗʰ 2022

Stress levels were high. It was suggested during one of many calls to crisis line that I speak with my GP about antidepressants. On the plus side, I was offered a trust deed in order to help pay off my debts. They were very understanding and said if I paid off half, they would erase the other half. This seemed fair as I would not be covering what Nikki had sponged from me over the years. Twelve addresses, three cars, countless furniture, storage costs... she had footed me with everything. Nobody wanted to move but her!

The problem is, I was now tied here at least until the debt was cleared in four years time, regardless of whether I managed to get into the girls life. At least she was honouring the Saturday phone call, even if she *did* cause at least two of them to end early. On one occasion, there was a witness. Thank you for coming forward.

Sunday, December 4th 2022

I discover Marnie on Instagram after reactivating my account. On a whim I sent a message telling her what had happened. She was rather shocked as she knew I was a gentle giant that would do anything for anybody. We spoke for quite sometime and I learned something interesting. All of the women in the refuge had been put there by social services for their protection... except one. Nikki had just turned up one night claiming she had been abused. She knew the system, and used it to her advantage. The refuge only helped re-home resident placed there by the services. Nikki's only option for housing was to get a job and rent one in the private sector, or fall pregnant and validate herself for social housing.

I was speechless. It's why she had been so keen on me. She had used me since day one as some kind of social and financial crash mat. Not just me, but our children as well. This realisation pushed me to the edge.

Monday, December 5th 2022

Even now, all genned up on covert narcissists. I am still bereaved for the person Nikki had portrayed herself as. This fake persona was my perfect companion.

Today would have been our seventh anniversary. Instead, I sit here in my apartment alone. It still doesn't feel like home despite looking ok. It is also the seventh 'month'iversary since I saw my children. There has been no word on the legal action for weeks. I do not feel any fulfilment in my work. I'm 450 miles away from friends and family to be by my girls which I cannot see. After she placed a restraining order on Paul, I dare not do anything. I don't like the swarm of bees in my head. I am on the phone to help centres in flood of tears. I gain an urge to end it all by taking an overdose. There are many pills in the first aid box.

One last call to the Samaritans saved my life. The gentleman I spoke to listened to my story, and I had told him about my own toxic mother and how she had moved me 200 miles from my father when I was only four years old. She had told me he had done bad things as well, but of course, I knew this was all lies now.

The Samaritan said, "You are not harming yourself tonight. Think about it Jim. You are not fighting this for you. You are fighting this because you do not want your daughters to be left to grow up with a toxic mother like you had as a child."

The psychological damage was done, but he was correct. I would NOT let my children grow up bereft of their father. Dear Samaritan, whoever you were, you hit the nail on the head!

Friday, December 16th 2022

The court papers had finally been served on Nikki. "YES!" First hearing in January.
But how would things go now?

Friday, 6th January 2023

I am granted three hours of access with the girls by the courts for each Saturday onwards. . This is an obstacle because living remotely the buses take long than this to arrive. I needed a miracle. That miracle was Brionny and Dennis. They so kindly gave us their lounge as a safe and warm meeting place out of the cold Scottish winter. They barely knew me but had supported me so much for the girls sake.

Nightmares, suicidal thoughts, and other antics from Nikki and her flying monkeys would still torment my soul. My biggest fear would be if Tanya still recognised me? She had barely turned three when I was emotionally coerced away.

She was first through the door with her arms in the air, a big smile and shouting "Daddy daddy daddy!" You can imagine how pleased I felt.

Friday, 3rd February 2023

Another hearing, another three hours on top. As kind as Brionny had been, I could not impose upon their day for six hours. The village hall committee offered me the hall at a discounted price temporarily. It was increased time which kept me going forwards, but I was still mentally beaten down. Janie for example, used her Facebook popularity to trash an entire charity just because I supported them. Prat.

I would return home from a night shift a few days later. Just as I was falling asleep there was a huge knock at the door. Two uniformed officer strode in saying Nikki had made allegations of harassment. Luckily I had seen this coming by the way she had treated paul. I presented them with all the proof I had and they left without a problem. Another attempt to make me look like the villain. This was very disorienting and did not help with my soul. It was a dirty trick she would try three times to intimidate me.

Friday, March 31st 2023

My time with the girls is increased yet again. This case seems endless but I stick to it for them. My time is reduced to 4 hours every two Saturday but... an overnight stay every other week! It gets better, but still isn't enough for me. I am their Daddy who they love dearly, not an uncle visiting weekly. Why is this taking so long?

My managers have had me called to the office. It is apparent my situation is taking its toll on my work performance. I'm overlooking things, or hurrying. They set up weekly counselling for me. It's only six weeks worth, but it shows they are looking out for me.

Nikki doesn't allow the girls to bring their beloved comfort blankets. This is a plan to make their stay with me too much for them no doubt? Ever concerned, Brionny sends a substitute which looks similar. This pleases Tanya so much. Everything goes perfectly.

Friday, July 21st 2023

This is when the fourth hearing takes place held by Sheriff Scott. Nikki's legal rep suggest I only get to see the girls fortnightly so that Nikki gets 'quality' time with the girls as well ad school days. What a ridiculous thing to come out with! All time with your children should be quality. Sheriff Scott reads out a statement from Casey.

"I love time with Daddy. We do painting, baking and play doh's. It's super fun time."
She added that at no point would she ever deny a father and child with such a close bond any contact and expresses her disappointment in both of our solicitors for not resolving this sooner.

Monday, July 8th 2024

It would be another year before the court action comes to a close. I have been granted three overnight stays our of four weeks on a Saturday, and virtually half of the school holidays. It is a far cry from the full custody I sought, but I have fought hard in the face of everything for over two years. I am sorry babies, Casey and Tanya. If you ever read this, please try to understand Daddy did everything he could, and just going forwards to be there for you was a fight I would do over again like any good parent would. When you are old enough, you can make a choice where to be, but I am pleased I am close by and there when my father had no opportunity to do this for me. I love you both xx

Knowing Your Narcissist

Narcissistic personality disorder is a mental condition in which people have an inflated sense of their own importance, a deep need for excessive attention and admiration, troubled relationships, and a lack of empathy for others. They are self-centred and prey on empathic people. Using coercive control to shift blame onto others by twisting words and telling untruths so that they do not have to accept responsibility for their own actions.

You may think you have the best partner in the world for years until what you supply them with runs out, and they turn on your overnight, socially disgracing you and making you doubt your own sanity.

YOU ARE NOT TO BLAME

Hello.

You are most likely experiencing the darkest time of your life right now. Am I right? Well, that's mainly because, at the time of writing this book, I was going through it as well. I will now share all the help I possibly can with you to overcome your own experience with a covertly narcissistic partner.

I must tell you, I hold no other qualification other than being a victim myself, and what I share with you has helped in my own recovery through this horrific experience. I cannot name my narc for legal reasons, but I will refer to her or them as Nex. (Narcissistic ex).

We shall first take a look at my personal experience as a blueprint to continue. For the most part, every experience is usually the same, just deployed differently. I do hope you find this book and everything in it incredibly useful, and I apologise for any typos, as I am not a good typist, just a working-class male. We Empaths must stick together.

For each book sold, I will donate the price of a tree sapling to the Plantfortheplanet.

Breaking up with a narcissist is a terrible journey. You realise that all along you have been living with someone's ego rather than their heart.

You will feel disoriented, depressed, angry, lonely, and, let's be honest, a little pathetic.

DON'T!

Ultimately, you will become stronger through healing than you could ever imagine, and you will not just be able to spot narcs in the future but also learn how to deal with them.

You are NOT alone! It is NOT your fault!

Signs a narcissist is finished with you

1. The love-bombing stage is over.

2. They devalue and criticise everything you do.

3. They ignore you or make themselves inaccessible to you.

4. They avoid spending time with you, especially in public.

5. They're irritated with you all the time.

6. They don't care when they see you crying.

7. They use gaslighting tactics.

8. They manipulate you into taking responsibility for their abusive behaviour.

9. When they talk about you, they drag your name through the mud, even after singing your praises for years.

10. They dogwhistle you. Another manipulative tactic.

So, you read my story? If you did, I will bet many of you can resonate with much of it.

11 Signs You Are Being Love-bombed

1, Something is moving too fast

2, Something feels too personal too quickly

3,Someone labels you partner after just a couple of dates.

4, Someone acts needy and demanding from day one.

5, Communication contains demands.

6, someone wants to rephrase what they've said to change your responses.

7, Someone wants to be rescued.

8, Someone refuses blame for any of their failed relationships.

9, Someone suddenly loves everything you love.

10, Someone's personality switches depending on who's around them.

11, Someone's attitude, beliefs, humour etc is not consistent.

Gaslighting

An evil form of covert manipulation where a narcissist or narc subtly targets the victim by making them question their mind, memory, and reality. Over two years on at the time of writing this book, I am receiving counselling, cognitive behavioural therapy and on antidepressants for the low mood and anxieties I endure.

5 Ways Narcissists Smear

1. Preemptively start a smear campaign by planting lies in the minds of others.

2. Paint themselves as the devoted, loving, innocent victim of you.

3. Twists stories and lies about your character, making sure to incorporate a grain of truth as a 'get out clause'.

4, lines up a replacement to use for future reputation management, supply, and triangulation. (the old man)

5. Discards you out of the blue. Flaunts a new supplier and uses your reactions as proof that you are the blame for all the relationship problems to anyone shallow-minded enough to believe.

I begged. I pleaded. I cried. Nothing I could say would now sway this operating-covert narcissist. She just stared at me sternly. The damage was done. The real person was out. Six and a half years to a mind explosion. Several wiser neighbours had witnessed her antics. They were encouraging me to stand my ground. I feel I maybe should have, but my brain had been programmed at the time to be convinced it was all my own doing, and if I didn't leave, I'd be thrown out. I had to think of my children first. I did what I thought was correct at the time.

I will now seek a court order as I heal and rebuild my life from the ground up. As I write this line, it has been 7 weeks since this happened. I have only just started going out again. Not for too long; it is now exhausting. But being indoors has given me some amazing opportunities to convince myself that none of this was my own fault. It was the workings of a cruel and savage personality that used people for her own ends before discarding them like a candy bar wrapper.

If you can relate to anything I have said so far, I bet you can. Punch the air and give me a loud "HELL YES!" before carrying on. You, my friend, are an empath like I am, and we are all targeted by narcissists because of our kind nature. We are the very same.

So what now?

I won't lie to you; this is going to be hard, and even I am expecting it to get worse before it gets better. Reports from the village tell me she is saying I left them penniless of my own accord. I would never leave my daughters voluntarily. Her flying monkeys have probably been suckered in by lies as well.

What are flying monkeys?

Flying monkeys are the collection of friends that the narcissist smears you with. They start viraling through their own connections, which spreads the narcissist slander of you without the narc in question getting their own hands dirty. They are also used by the narc to spy on their victims in the aftermath. They could have even been your own friends up until the smearing. But their lack of judgement says more about them than you.

My Nex has between 6 and 10 flying monkeys, and none of them really know me that well. She chose wisely but didn't realise I like to speak out about problems. Her catchphrase is "I don't want the world to know my business."

I can see why now!

Firstly, block all those as soon as you work out who they are. To be fair, they have been fooled as much as you have, so don't go pursuing any vendettas. They made their choice of friend; you don't need them in your life.

Secondly, that new supply your narc is with has taken the bait just as you did. More fool them. Do not have a go at them or fight them; it'll make you look like the bad person, which is what Narc wants. Do not try to warn them or their family. That could be seen as stalking or obsession in court. Let time sort them out. One day they will be left standing too, or tell the narc to get lost. Now, if they do tell the narc to get lost, there is a chance the narc will return to you and do something called hoovering.

Hoovering

Hoovering is the sneaky way narcissists try to get you back when they have nowhere else to turn. Do NOT fall for it. They are only going to sucker you in again. They may say or text you some sort of apology, tell you they are going to change, or even start love-bombing you again, at least in a literal sense. Be strong. You now have the power to tell them, "No!"

The very best contact you have with that narc, and one of the things that pisses them off immensely, is saying nothing at all. Cut off all communication, no matter how hard that might be or how your head may be. You are now in power! Easy as that. They will only try to make it hard for you next time.

This may be difficult if you have children. You need to ensure that you only speak to the children, and if they do not let you, get people involved. Mediators, Social Services, all the way up to a court order. Go for it, and don't let the narc know, or they will try to guilt-trip you for wasting people's time.

Now, what can you do with this power? You can learn about narcissists and their behaviours. Continue reading this book for a layman's example of help, but I would also fully recommend the videos on YouTube and Facebook by the incredible Rebecca Zung. She is an expert on narcissistic behaviour and deals with it every day in her work role, (Authors note- and my god, she's pretty.)

The truth always comes out in the end. Lies are just temporary delays to the inevitable.

Now it's time to train yourself up. You have already seen a few ways to spot narcissistic traits in people. Let's look at some things you can say to shut them down in conversation should the narc start getting argumentative with you. Once again, the best response is no response. They hate themselves, and the only way they can justify their actions is by trying to make you feel hurt in their place. They cannot take being wrong or accept blame, and they only listen to argue back. Here are a couple of phrases to help you out when they are being confrontational with you: Be careful, though, as these may trigger narcissistic rage.

Phrases to shut down a narcissist.

1. "Your Anger Is Not My Responsibility"

This resets the playing field so that they cannot make you a source of their narcissist supply to soothe their emotions. To add, this statement is very grounding and draws a very clear boundary between what you will and will not be responsible for.

2. "I Can't Control How You Feel About Me"

This sets the precedent that their emotions are their responsibility and that their reaction won't change your behavior. This statement also reinforces that you only have control over yourself and others have control over themselves, and you will not be made to feel responsible for others' emotions.

3. "I Hear What You're Saying"

This allows the narcissist to feel heard, which might be all you want to say if you want to de-escalate and not further discuss the point of contention. This statement may be one of the fastest ways to deescalate a narcissist because feeling heard is a common desire everyone has. While you may not agree with what the narcissist is saying, simply stating that you hear what is being said can be enough in the moment.

4. "I'm Sorry You Feel That Way"

You can feel sorry for someone else without being sorry about your boundaries, which is important when arguing with a narcissist. This makes the narcissist responsible for their emotions while potentially helping them be heard so they don't further escalate an issue.

5. "Everything Is Okay"

This helps to make it clear to the narcissist that this will pass and they are okay or going to be okay. Given that narcissists have no self-awareness, it's likely they cannot reconcile high conflict or intense emotions. Saying things will be okay gives them the reassurance and/or validation they don't know they need.

6. "We Both Have a Right to Our Own Opinions"

This makes it clear that they can have their opinion, and making sure it's clear that you know their words are opinions, not facts. To add to that, it's important to make this statement so they know they are also being heard and to reset the playing field of the conversation.

Narcissists will want to feel superior and be in control of the conversation, but stating this makes it clear that you won't allow that to happen, but you can respect that they are going to have their own opinions as well.

7. "I Can Accept How You Feel"

Don't fight a narcissist when you disagree with them, because you won't convince them or change their mind. Simply saying that you accept their opinion or how they feel without fighting back cuts off their supply.

8. "I Don't Like How You're Speaking To Me So I Will Not Engage"

Saying this sets a boundary. They feed off of triggering you, so knowing that you won't participate in a fight will cut off their supply. For this to work, it's important that you don't cave in when the narcissist inevitably persists in engaging you.

9. "I Am not Going to Argue Anymore"

Very clear message that you will not continue to engage in an unproductive fight. Again, for this to work, it's important that you stand your ground and walk away.

10. "I am Capable of Doing What I Want Regardless of What you Think"

This makes it clear that you are okay with your perspective, that it's not changing, and that you are also making it clear that their opinion in this situation won't shape your behaviour.

11. "I Understand"

This makes it clear that you are indeed understanding what they are saying. You are not stating that you agree, but that you understand. Narcissists have a deep need to feel understood, heard, and seen, so stating that you are understanding will help a narcissist feel less agitated.

12. "We Can Agree to Disagree"

Like a few other phrases, for this to work,

it's important you double down on this and don't feed into the temptation to engage in an argument. You may feel like you want to prove or convince the narcissist of something, but that will not work. Simply agreeing to disagree gives the narcissist the knowledge that their opinions and perspectives were heard.

13. "I See Where You Are Coming From"

This phrase helps the narcissist feel understood. It helps them to feel that their thought process makes sense, even if you don't agree with their interpretation of it.

14. "I Want To Share How I Feel"

Using "I" statements is always best, as it keeps the blame off of others and makes you the owner of how you feel. Sharing how you feel can humanise the interaction, and though the narcissist may not care, it's possible they will ease off if they feel you are interpreting yourself as a victim. They will likely then try to use tactics to portray themselves as victims, in which case the anger will likely dissipate and de-escalation will be made easier.

15. "Your Perspective Is Interesting"

This statement makes it appear that their perspective is neither bad nor good, but interesting. It allows the narcissist to sit in their feelings, trying to understand, and makes them pause. The pause can be a good moment to use another phrase to further calm down the situation.

16. "Can We Aim To be Respectful In Our Conversation?"

This phrase used as a question is more rhetorical, but when used literally, it can level the conversation, so it is not so emotionally charged.

Credit to -choosingtherapy.com

Additionally, narcissists hate the word, "Whatever." They spend their every moment cancelling out your feelings and emotions, and they go scatty when you do it back with this one word. "Whatever."

When a narcissist can no longer control you, they will try to control how others see you.

Other things that can cripple a narcissist are phrases like these. (Remember this can turn them nasty as well.)

You are a failure, loser, coward etc.
This completely robs their ego and self-importance exposing the truth. The truth hurts, none moreso than a narc.

I don't believe you.
This really sets them on edge. You are invalidating all that comes out of their mouths, and rightly so.

I'm too busy/weary for you.
This sounds like you are ready to move on. Narcissists hate 'tone', you could be quite scathing if you say it correctly.

I just delete your emails and texts.
A sure sign to the narc that you do not hold them as important anymore and invalidate their life.

The Healing Process

This isn't quick and easy, despite all these pointers I am sharing with you. From day one, the trauma headache will feel like your head is about to explode. Seek the company of a friend or family member if you have children. You will also be ruminating. This is when your thoughts bombard you with the hows, whys, what ifs and did I's. The simple answer, once again, is no. You have not done anything wrong. You are the victim of a liar, a fraudster, a charlatan, and possibly a cheater. You have nothing to be ashamed of. You are not alone!

However, the world may feel like it has turned to paper, the air may seem thin, and your senses may be heightened to the point where loud noises really hurt your ears. You wish to be in an empty room with four walls, as seeing the distance makes you feel like your happiness is far away. This is natural, I am afraid. You are healing from the biggest of emotional shocks. Be a warrior. Be a survivor.

Write down everything. Keep a diary, and record any calls. Do not make them public, despite how much you might want to. It'll make you look like you are obsessive or stalking. You must distance yourself, and if you want to get sweet revenge, thrive. Find your footing once again in whatever way you can. Maybe a better job, going back to education—anything but ultimately showing the Narc that you can survive without them and will not pander to them anymore. Remember, do NOT let them hoover you again. You will need constant distraction, immerse yourself in something you enjoy or your work. You may find the strength to go out for a small walk. A little at a time will turn into a lot in the long run. Once the trauma and rapid thoughts disperse, you will be seeing things clearly enough to smile and laugh again, and more importantly, move on.

There are many options to help you through it. Remember the charity Samaritans? While they cannot do anything practical, they will listen if you need to chat. There are social media communities that will embrace you, as the members have had similar experiences as you. Sometimes, it's better to speak with a stranger, as they are unbiased.

'The truth will always come out in the end, no matter how hard anyone tries to hide or stop it. Lies are just temporary delays of the inevitable.'

I hope my write-up has offered you some positive help, and if even just one piece of it makes sense to you, I am sure you will fight your way through your experience as I have also done this past few weeks. Bless you, stay strong and remember... you are better than they will ever be, and worth more than they can ever deserve!

Post Narcissistic Discard Help

Hopefully you will have already sought help from your closest family/friends. Always trust that gut instinct. I came so close to being homeless and all of my possessions stolen. Speak out, cover yourself.

As mentioned earlier, knowledge is power. Do your research on narcississtic personality disorder and other areas of what is know as the Dark Triad. Rebecca Zung and Doctor Ramani are leaders on the YouTube video side. Also check out Danish Bashir and Melanie Tonia Evans on Facebook.

Make sure you arrange your needs. If you need to go on the sick, your GP will sign you off for up to a month if your life has become impacted with stress and anxiety. He may even offer medicine to help. You will not feel like it at first, but your sleep will improve at least a little. There is no telling how long this will last depending on the damage done. I met a gentleman who has been suffering for nine years, as he is still tied to his ex partner by their child.

DOCUMENT EVERYTHING. It will be your proof. Keep emails, record calls, screenshot texts etc.

I am in the UK. If you do not live their you will need to find the equivalents of these next suggestions.

Helplines:

Samaritans 116123

The Calm Zone 0800 585858

Online Help:

My Black Dog

www.nhs.uk (search for an anxiety test)

www.bulliesout.com

womansaid.org.uk

Parental Aienation

There is little more revolting than a toxic parent who alienates their children from the other parent without good reason. (Violence, substance abuse, etc)

In this day and age a narcissistic parent will delight in torturing you this way, not just by blocking contact, but also by telling the children horrible things about that parent so the child's relationship will end up broken. This type of poisonous mind-washing also destroys the child's relationship with their greater family, aunt's, grandparents, cousins and the like. Act swiflty. All too often people hesitate about getting Court involved. For the child's sake, do it! Don't let the toxic parent promise you a better tomorrow. Take the reigns back which they stole from you in the first place with their manipulation. Take legal action if you can. A family law solicitor will help you arrange Legal Aid if you are on low income.

Also, check out www.paawareness.co.uk

Get Involved

Mix with other people going through the same plight. They will become like a new right arm for your battle ahead. Stay active once the adjustment trauma has worn off. I was lucky enough to become involved with an amazing project by actress Theresa Godly. Her short film, The Stranger I Love, is an amazing insight into her own personal battle with parental alienation. If you get chance to see this, please do.

Reach Out

If your experience has left you in financial difficulty, contact Stepchange or Carrington Dean who will be able to keep the debt collectors away May sure they know your story. Even the Job Centre will sympathise if you tell them what has happened.

If your mental health has been effected so

badly then you may be able to apply for something called Limited Capability For Work And Related Activity (LCWRA). Search on the government website to arrange an assessment. If working, let your boss know and ask if there are any in-house counselling services or occupational health branches within the company.

IT IS TIME TO LOOK AFTER YOU!

Well readers, that's it from me. I hope this book can enlighten and encourage many of you. As I draw it to a close I am 27 months along. Court has just finished, I am still on meds and therapy for the psychological damage, but I am far stronger than I was. I see my children, and just wait for the next drama a day at a time. Narc's will do that, but I will NEVER back down. Neither should you. Nikki has spent thousands of John's money. Maybe he will see the light, but for now, me, and all of her past victims are now friends and support each other.

On your side,

love Jim

Printed in Great Britain
by Amazon